AF489835

# TABLE OF CONTENTS


**INTRODUCTION**.................................................................. **4**

**QUIZ 1** .......................................................................... **5**

**QUIZ 2** .......................................................................... **7**

**QUIZ 3** .......................................................................... **9**

**QUIZ 4** ........................................................................ **11**

**QUIZ 5** ........................................................................ **13**

**QUIZ 6** ........................................................................ **15**

**QUIZ 7** ........................................................................ **17**

**QUIZ 8** ........................................................................ **19**

**QUIZ 9** ........................................................................ **21**

**QUIZ 10** ....................................................................... **23**

**QUIZ 11** ....................................................................... **25**

**QUIZ 12** ....................................................................... **27**

**QUIZ 13** ....................................................................... **29**

**QUIZ 14** ....................................................................... **31**

**QUIZ 15** .......................................................................................... 33

**QUIZ 16** .......................................................................................... 35

**QUIZ 17** .......................................................................................... 37

**QUIZ 18** .......................................................................................... 39

**QUIZ 19** .......................................................................................... 41

**QUIZ 20** .......................................................................................... 43

**QUIZ 21** .......................................................................................... 45

**QUIZ 22** .......................................................................................... 47

**QUIZ 23** .......................................................................................... 49

**QUIZ 24** .......................................................................................... 51

**QUIZ 25** .......................................................................................... 53

**QUIZ 26** .......................................................................................... 55

**QUIZ 27** .......................................................................................... 57

**QUIZ 28** .......................................................................................... 59

**QUIZ 29** .......................................................................................... 61

**QUIZ 30** .......................................................................................... 63

**QUIZ 31** ................................................................................ **65**

**QUIZ 32** ................................................................................ **67**

**QUIZ 33** ................................................................................ **69**

**QUIZ 34** ................................................................................ **71**

**QUIZ 35** ................................................................................ **73**

**QUIZ 36** ................................................................................ **75**

**QUIZ 37** ................................................................................ **77**

**QUIZ 38** ................................................................................ **79**

**QUIZ 39** ................................................................................ **81**

**QUIZ 40** ................................................................................ **83**

# Introduction

As a matter of fact, that humans living rhythm has been promoted immensely with the upgrading of neo-technology and hi-technology. However, reading books is still maintained as a healthy habit and it always proves its indispensable roles in our modern life. During pre-teen years, children are transitioning into secondary education and their lives inevitably become busier with homework, clubs, sports, and extra-curricular activities. This is also a time in which children are seeking greater independence. The main purpose of this book is to bring us more enjoyment as a family by asking one another mind-boggling riddles, that are a whole heap of fun. We believe it's really important to set quality time aside to stretch the mind and imagination and build bonds as a family.

As parents, we've found that through fun riddles our children have learned many educational and life-skills without realizing that this crucial learning is taking place. Three of the top skills that we believe riddles promote and encourage are the following:

1. The Ability to Think Outside the Box: Riddles help children apply logic and creativity to reach a conclusion. Children can learn literal and non-literal meanings of words. Children can learn to use their imaginations and become more inventive.

2. Problem Solving: In order to solve problems, children need to be able to find solutions, resolve issues, and develop creative options.

3. Enhancing Vocabulary: Unfamiliar words present parents with the perfect opportunity to encourage kids to use a dictionary. Parents can then encourage them to use the words in sentences to ensure that they understand their meaning. The riddles will certainly help to place new words in context in a fun way.

We hope you and your family has as much fun working through these riddles as our family did. Best luck!

# QUIZ 1

1. You're driving around in a fancy car. Which of your tires don't move when you turn right onto a street?
2. You can find me in socks, scarves, and mittens, but you can also find me in the paws of a playful kitten. What am I?
3. A cat has three; a dog has three; but a school has six. What is it?
4. What goes up when the rain comes down?
5. I'm short when I'm old but tall when I'm young. What am I?
6. Mike is a butcher. He is really big. He's 7 feet tall, wears really big boots, and he has a big, bushy beard. What does he weigh?
7. I have a brother beside me. However, we run the same speed; but we can never meet each other. What am I?
8. There is one in every corner and two in every room. What?
9. What is the four-digit number, without zeros, while the first and fourth digits are similar numbers, half of the sum of the second and the fourth digit is the second number, while the last digit is half of the sum of the first and the third numbers, consider that the sum of all digits is 24?
10. A man was driving a black car with no lights. The moon showed no light. A cat was in the middle of the road, how did he know?

# ANSWERS QUIZ 1

1. Your spare tire
2. Yarn
3. Letters
4. An umbrella
5. Candle
6. Meat! Mike is a butcher so he weighs meat.
7. Wheels
8. Letter O
9. 6,666
10. It was daytime.

# QUIZ 2

1. I have keys, without locks and I can unlock your soul. What am I?
2. What is the number that five is more than 1/5 of 1/10 of 1/4 of a thousand?
3. I can be found on the internet or the newspaper or even a calendar. I can be rather expensive, but can also be cheap and affordable. I can be a treat for someone special. You can have me in the park, a movie theatre or even a restaurant. However, you have to be two to enjoy me. Who am I?
4. You can never do without me- What am I?
5. What would you say if you met a ghost in your bedroom?
6. One department planned a farewell meeting to bid goodbyes to their retiring workmates. It was calculated that each person must pay $30. "We are lucky that there are not five lesser of us to split the bill, either way it would be $10 more for each of us", said one of them. How much did the meeting cost and how many of them split the bill?
7. During what month people sleep the least?
8. What gets broken if it isn't kept?
9. What number has all letters in alphabetical order when spelled out?
10. Dirk makes shoes with no leather using fire, water, air, and earth. Every customer orders 2 pairs of shoes. Who is Dirk?

# ANSWERS QUIZ 2

1. Piano
2. 10(1000÷4=250÷10=25÷5=5+5=10).
3. A date
4. Water
5. Hi Boo?
6. Twenty people split a $600-dollar bill.
7. February, there are only 28/29 days
8. A promise
9. Forty
10. HE'S A BLACKSMITH WHO MAKES HORSESHOES.

# QUIZ 3

1. They never come out during the day because light is harmful to them. If you decide to wait for them at night, they might catch you and bite on your neck. What are they?
2. I weaken everyone for hours each day. I can show you strange and wonderful sights while you're with me. I take you by night and let you go during the day. You don't mind having me, but you will suffer without me.
3. I can die despite not being alive. What am I?
4. Men walk over it but boats go under it. What is it?
5. Snap, Pop and crackle were all very scared. What happened?
6. I am object you use which is 6 letters-word, but if you remove the first letter and replace it with "c" people hate it- What am I?
7. What has one foot but no body?
8. A donkey is on 20ft chain and what an orange that is 22ft away. How can the donkey get the orange?
9. I am something I state the correct time perfectly twice a day- What am I?
10. They have wings and are very tiny. They are however very scary and only the very brave can go near them and even touch them. You will always find them hanging upside down and mostly in caves. Who are they?

# ANSWERS QUIZ 3

1. Vampires
2. Sleep
3. A battery.
4. Bridge
5. They heard that a serial killer was on the loose
6. Basket (replace the first letter with C, it's casket)
7. Ruler
8. The chain wasn't tied to anything
9. Stopped Time
10. Bats

# QUIZ 4

1. When should you wear a helmet and a seatbelt to dinner?
2. I have plenty of keys but don't have any doors, I have space but there are no rooms, I allow you to enter, but you can never leave. What am I?
3. Noah brought 100 pairs of animals onto the ark. By the time Noah sent the dove out, each pair had had two babies. How many were there then? 399, the dove left.
4. How did the beach greet the tide as it came in?
5. I named myself, I cannot be seen, the only organ that I ever named in history. What am I?
6. What room in the house isn't for ghosts?
7. A book with one page, you read through a whole year, what am I?
8. How did the tiger feel after eating Ellen De Generes and Jimmy Kimmel?
9. There are three numbers that will have the same answer, either they are added or multiplied together. What is it?
10. Which number when added to 5/4 gives the same result as when it is multiplied 5/4?

# ANSWERS QUIZ 4

1. When you're on a crash diet.
2. Keyboard.
3. 399, the dove left.
4. Hi! Long time no sea (see)!
5. Brain
6. None.
7. Calendar
8. Funny
9. 1,2 and 3
10. 5

# QUIZ 5

1. What must take a bow before it can speak?
2. What is it that given one, you'll have either two or none?
3. What is that over the head and under the hat?
4. Bamtaramushkabalurzeekhanz...how do you spell it?
5. It has a jacket without pants. What is it?
6. What flies when it born, lies while it is alive, and runs when it dies?
7. You always feel like sharing me when you have me, but if you do it, you will lose me. What am I?
8. Sometimes it is a girl, other times it is a boy. Sometimes, it is porcelain while other times it is plastic. But, it is always a toy that you can play with.
9. I can't go in no direction other than up and down. I am stuck, moving in a building. What am I?
10. What is seen in the water and in the sky? It is part of the rainbow and can be in your eye.

# ANSWERS QUIZ 5

1. Violin
2. Choice
3. Hair
4. I and T ("it").
5. Book
6. Snowflake
7. Secret
8. A doll
9. Elevator
10. Blue

# QUIZ 6

1. What smells the most in the kitchen?
2. I am a soulless, cold creature. If I feel heat in me, it will kill me. What am I?
3. What are you likely to get when you cross some alcohol and lightning bug?
4. What has four wings but cannot fly and uses the wind but does not know why?
5. While two twins are in the room together with a King and Queen, there weren't any adults there. Why?
6. What fish is a celebrity?
7. What is all over the house?
8. What excites girls when they watch Bridesmaids, Mermaids, Pretty Woman and Legally Blonde?
9. I am something that you can make and break even with touching. What am I?
10. Why did the monster eat everyone else, but not the crazy person?

# ANSWERS QUIZ 6

1. Nose
2. Snowman
3. A light ale
4. Windmill
5. All of them are beds.
6. Starfish
7. Roof
8. They are romantic comedies
9. A promise.
10. He was allergic to nuts

# QUIZ 7

1. What do goblins sing in the shower?
2. The longer you write the shorter I go- What am I?
3. Why did the mummy never make any friends?
4. Samuel was walking in the middle of a desert when suddenly, it started to rain. However, he had no umbrella or hat. Yet, not a single hair on his head got wet from the rain storm. How did this happen? Answer: Samuel was bald!
5. How can you turn a novel into a stream?
6. What word starts with "E", ends with "E", but only has one letter? It is not the letter "E".
7. What is smarter than a talking donkey?
8. What falls but never breaks - and what breaks but never falls?
9. My back is on the ground but my 100 feet is in the air. How - what am I?
10. There was one night, a prince and a princess went into a castle. No one can be found in the castle during that time, and there was no sight of anyone who came inside nor outside. In the morning, there were three who came out of the place. Who were they?

# ANSWERS QUIZ 7

1. Rhythm and boos
2. Pencil
3. She was too wrapped in herself
4. Samuel was bald!
5. Turn "book" into "brook"
6. Envelope
7. A spelling bee
8. Night and day
9. a centipede lying on its back on the ground, with all 100 feet waving in the air.
10. The knight (nigh), the king, and the queen

# QUIZ 8

1. On a sunny day, the captain docked the ship in the harbor. The ship began to sink, there were no natural calamities, no storm or anything. Everything was completely fine, but it sank right away. Why?
2. What language can you speak without saying a word out loud?
3. Name all the numbers from 1 - 100, which have the letter "A" in their spelling.
4. A man made a promise to his village that one day he would be able to walk on water. Each day he tried, it was warm and sunny, but each day he failed. One day he woke up and it was cold outside. It had been cold all night and he knew that today was his chance. He did it. He walked on water in front of his whole village. How did he do this?
5. You put me in the soil to keep me alive and dig me up when I wither. What am I?
6. I am something I sleep at night. What am I?
7. This won't fit in the biggest pot in the kitchen. What is it?
8. My name is Yoda. I live in a house. I have four dogs living along with me. Their names are Sky, Nighty, Aftie, and Brownie. Who do you think the fifth dog is?
9. What kind of cup doesn't hold water?
10. There's a name on me that I do not own. People cry at my sight and stay beside me day and night. What am I?

# ANSWERS QUIZ 8

1. The submarine captain ordered his crew to dive
2. Body language
3. None
4. It was so cold overnight that the water had frozen over. He was walking on a frozen lake.
5. Plant
6. Living Thing
7. The lid
8. Yoda.
9. Cupcake
10. Tombstone

# QUIZ 9

1. What word can be written forward, backward or upside down?
2. There are 3 stoves in front of you and you only have 1 match. The first stove is made of glass. The second stove is made of wood and the third stove is made of bricks. Which do you light up first?
3. What do you get when you cross a snowman and a witch?
4. I can either be in a hook or beside a book, what am I?
5. What is the word that even in plain sight remains hidden?
6. You throw my outside, you eat what's in it and you throw what's within it. What am I?
7. Name consecutive three days without using the word Monday, Tuesday, Wednesday, Thursday, Friday, Saturday and Sunday.
8. When you're asked this question, you can't honestly answer with a yes. What is it?
9. They can swim as well as fish, and are slow as turtles. They hang and live on trees like monkeys. Who are they?
10. What is full of holes but still holds water? Sponge

# ANSWERS QUIZ 9

1. Noon
2. You light the match first.
3. You get a cold spell
4. Worm
5. Hidden
6. Corn
7. Yesterday, today, and tomorrow.
8. Are you asleep?
9. Sloths
10. Sponge

# QUIZ 10

1. A cloud was my mother, but I didn't stay with her for very long. The wind is my father, but he pushed us away. My son is the cool stream, and he is the reason I exist. I fall once in my life before I sleep in the earth one last time. What am I?
2. I have four legs but cannot walk. I hold food but I can't eat. What am I?
3. The more of me you have, the longer you live. The more you experience me, the less you have left. What am I?
4. The more you use me the more I get reduced, the more I do anything you want- What am I?
5. A man was sitting in a car when he saw in front of him a gold door, a silver door, and a bronze door. Which door will he open first?
6. Which cheese is made backward?
7. What is lighter than what it is made of? Ice
8. I am not alive, but I have five fingers. What am I?
9. While it doesn't have legs and bones, it will eventually walk around after being kept warm for a period of time.
10. Some call them their Romeo, some call them their world and others call them their superhero. They are very strong and also very sweet. They buy you gifts, open doors for you, take you out on dates and protect you. Who are they?

# ANSWERS QUIZ 10

1. Rain
2. Table
3. Heartbeat
4. Candle
5. Car door
6. Edam
7. Ice
8. A glove
9. An egg.
10. Boyfriends and husbands

# QUIZ 11

1. How many letters does the Greek alphabet contain?
2. Every girl enjoys a regular treat of this. I come in red, yellow and pink colors. I smell very nice but sometimes when you pick me you have to be very careful or I will bite you. Who am I?
3. The blue house is beside the blueberry patch, the red house is beside the strawberry fields, and the yellow house is beside the banana trees. Where is the white house? Washington D.C
4. It's very fancy and very shiny. Every girl, young and old, wants to have it. It is a perfect gift idea from a boy that really likes a girl. What is it?
5. I have six letters, remove one letter, and there are only twelve that remains. What am I?
6. I can travel the world just by staying in one spot. What am I?
7. I go around in circles, around in directions, never complain wherever I'm led. What am I?
8. How is an island like the letter "T"?
9. How is your mother's sister's brother-in-law related to you?
10. It is old and has run for a long time. It doesn't move at all. It has a mighty loud roar but no mouth or throat. It is the true beauty and power of nature. What is it?

# ANSWERS QUIZ 11

1.  16. The (3) Greek (5) alphabet (8) equals 16 letters.
2.  Roses
3.  Washington D.C
4.  Jewels
5.  Dozens
6.  A stamp.
7.  Wheel
8.  It's in the middle of water
9.  He's your father.
10. Waterfall

# QUIZ 12

1. You find yourself alone in a dark room and you have a matchstick and a matchbook. There are three objects near you: an oil lamp, a candle and a piece of firewood. Which of these things will you light first?
2. How short is this riddle's correct answer?
3. Their goal in life is to save princesses. They are invisible and they eat stars as their favorite delicacy. They are very jumpy and go through the mushroom kingdom. They are said to be originally from Italy.
4. I look at you, you stare back at me. I have three eyes, yet I see nothing. I send you commands every time I blink. You always obey me, jail is where you'll be if you don't follow me. What am I?
5. Which is cheaper: bringing your Mother twice to the same movie or bringing 2 friends once to a movie?
6. What am I?
7. What is the last thing you take off before bed?
8. The witch has a broomstick; the jack o'lantern has a candle. So what does a vampire have?
9. Draw a line on the paper, using a pen, make the line longer without even touching it.
10. I am as light as a feather, but the biggest, strongest person cannot hold me for 10 minutes.

# ANSWERS QUIZ 12

1. The matchstick.
2. How short.
3. Super Mario
4. Traffic Lights
5. Bringing 2 friends to a movie once, because you'll only pay for 3 people while bringing your Mom twice to a movie will make you pay for 4 people.
6. A question
7. Your feet
8. A bloodhound
9. You draw a shorter line next to it, and your first line becomes the longer line.
10. Breath

# QUIZ 13

1. What is the best way to fix a jack-o-lantern?
2. What word stars with IS, with the ending AND, and has LA in the center?
3. When a dog catcher catches 20 dogs in a week, how does he get paid?
4. What number gives the same answer when it is added to one and a half and when it is multiplied by the same number that is given?
5. Take me for a spin and I will make you cool, use me in winter and you are a fool. What am I?
6. We are a family of 12 members. I am the second. I am also the youngest in our family. Who am I?
7. What is the name given to a funny skeleton that makes you giggle and laugh?
8. I am crushed, I am thrashed, I am clogged and I am also given or kept. Whatever I go through, I always remain the same, I am always whole.
9. I am something people leave me in the morning and come back to me at night. What am I?
10. What food also sounds like it does when I see a ghost?

# ANSWERS QUIZ 13

1. Use a pumpkin patch
2. Island
3. By the pound
4. 3
5. Fan
6. February. A year has 12 months. February is the 2nd month and has the least days.
7. A funny bone
8. A heart
9. Bed
10. Ice cream (I scream)

# QUIZ 14

1. How many tickles can make an octopus laugh?
2. What's higher than the king?
3. A rooster laid an egg outside of its nest. How can the rooster put the egg back on its own nest?
4. There are 20 people in one classroom. You start counting everyone but realizes that there are only 19. You count again but keep getting the same result. What seems to be the problem?
5. It was brought to life by using electricity. It is made up of different body parts with bolts in the neck and its skin yellow. What is it?
6. This bet can never be won. What is it?
7. What is it that has four legs, one head, and a foot?
8. What lies in a tunnel of darkness? That can only attack when pulled back?
9. There was once a very popular skeleton who was a detective. What was his name?
10. Who is always the hottest person at all the Halloween parties?

# ANSWERS QUIZ 14

1. Ten tickles (tentacles, get it?).
2. Crown
3. It can't, because roosters don't lay eggs.
4. You need to count yourself.
5. Frankenstein's monster
6. Alphabet
7. Bed
8. Bullet
9. Sherlock bones
10. The devil

# QUIZ 15

1. If strawberry jam has jelly, you have family, and a pencil has a paper, what do skeletons have?
2. I am the favorite drink down south. With just three (3) letters in my name, I can lose the last two and still sound the same
3. It is a hairy creature and it does not like people. If ever you come across it, you should run very fast. You are only a little safe, if you have a gun that has silver bullets. What is this creature?
4. Giving it to someone undeserving is disgusting but taking it for yourself is considered to be honorable. If it were a game, nobody will win. What is it?
5. What can be full, but never spills and can be half, but is never cut?
6. When I was 4 years old, my sister was half my age. Today I am 15 years old. How old is my brother?
7. A farmer hires some help to carry grain to his barn. The farmer carried one sack of grain to the barn while his helper carried only two sacks. Who did the most work? Read the sentence carefully before you answer.
8. What in the world can be half of an elephant?
9. What is very red, juicy, delicious, and could be equally poisonous, if it was given to you by the wicked woman?
10. Pronounced as one letter, but you write me as. I can be double or single, I may be black, blue, and gray, and I'm read from both ends and either way. What am I?

# ANSWERS QUIZ 15

1. No-body
2. Tea
3. A werewolf
4. Blame.
5. Moon
6. 13 years old.
7. The farmer did the most work. He carried a sack of grain while the helper just carried two sacks. They were empty.
8. "ELEP" and "HANT"
9. Snow white's Apple
10. Eye

# QUIZ 16

1. You are driving a bus. At the first stop, two women get on. At the second stop, three men get on and one woman gets off. At the third stop, a mom gets on with her three kids. It's raining outside and the bus is bright green. Do you know what color the bus driver's hair is?

2. You can't see it, and you can't feel it. It can't be heard or smelled. It lies behind the stars, in deep caves under the hills, and empty holes it fills. It's the last thing you see because with it, you can't see at all. What is it?

3. A prisoner is told "if you tell a lie we will hang you, if you tell the truth we will shoot you". What can he say to save himself?

4. When is a man like a snake?

5. I can end up either deep in a book or pierced through a hook. What am I?

6. I devour everything and people never think I'm dangerous, what am I?

7. What can go through towns and over hills without moving? Road

8. It is small, scary and goes around zipping at night. What is it?

9. It is a body part that you give wholly to someone you like. However, it can be broken and that aches, throbs and even bleeds without any visible blood. What is it?

10. I always answer to your call, but I can be inaudible. What am I?

# ANSWERS QUIZ 16

1. You are the bus driver, what color id your hair?
2. The dark
3. You will hang me.
4. When is a man like a snake? When he's rattled.
5. A worm.
6. Time
7. Road
8. A bat in a bat mobile
9. A heart
10. Echo

# QUIZ 17

1. Fill in the missing numbers in the following series: 101 99 102 98 103 97? ?
2. A spider has $28 with it; an ant has $21 while the chicken has $7 with it. How much money will a dog have?
3. What kind of fish chases a mouse?
4. What snack can an invisible man have?
5. What grows when fed but dies when watered? Fire
6. A thief is condemned to be executed. He must choose between three different rooms. One room is full of blazing hot fires and feels like a furnace. Another is full of murderers who have loaded pistols, and the third is full of dragons, who haven't eaten in 2 years. Which room is the safest for the thief? Answer: The third. The dragons are dead, because they haven't eaten in two years!
7. I'm flat when you never use me, I'm fat if you do. I release gas when you poke into me, what am I?
8. You can hear me, but you can never touch nor see me. What am I?
9. He flies around with bows and arrows. However, when he makes shots, he does no harm. Instead of pain, all you feel is a lot of joy. Who is this guy?
10. How can you go for 5 days without sleep and feel and act normal?

# ANSWERS QUIZ 17

1. 104 and 96. There are really 2 series in one, one starts at 101 and counts up; the other starts at 99 and counts down 5.
2. $14 ($3.50 per leg).
3. Catfish
4. Evaporated milk.
5. Fire
6. The third. The dragons are dead, because they haven't eaten in two years!
7. A balloon
8. Voice
9. Cupids
10. You sleep in the evenings.

# QUIZ 18

1. What goes further the slower it goes?
2. Dexter was 25 years old 2 days ago. Next year, he will be 28 years old. How can this be?
3. What gets harder to catch the faster you run?
4. I live in the water, but I hate the water. What am I?
5. What did Adam and Eve lack that everyone else has?
6. You look away and pretend you don't know me when you release me, maybe because I always send your friends away. What am I?
7. What fills a room but takes up no space?
8. I always tell the truth even if I don't say and hear anything. What am I?
9. What gets served but never eaten? Tennis Ball
10. It does not matter how young or how old they are. It does not matter if they are either steady or broken. They are very protective and caring and can do anything for the ones they love. Who are they?

# ANSWERS QUIZ 18

1. Money
2. Today is January 1. Two days ago was December 30, and his 26th birthday was yesterday, December 30. On December 30 this year, he turns 27 and next year, he turns 28 on December 30.
3. Breath
4. Salt
5. Parents
6. Fart
7. Light
8. A mirror.
9. Tennis Ball
10. Your girlfriend or girlfriend

# QUIZ 19

1. What is the five-letter word that becomes shorter when you add two more letters?
2. Where can you find an ocean with no water and towns without people?
3. Five years ago, you were five years younger. In 5 years, you will be 5 years older than now. What will you be in 10 years?
4. He's a man that's heartless and cold. If you try to give him warmth, he'll slowly die. What is he?
5. What type of house weighs the least?
6. Two people went for a walk on a cloudy day, but they forgot to bring their umbrellas. Why aren't they getting wet?
7. What is red, blue, purple and green that no one can reach, not even the queen?
8. What needs you to answer it but it cannot ask a question?
9. It is a beast that is believed to have just one horn. I am mystical and, therefore, very difficult to catch. You know me?
10. What do you call a man who does not have all his fingers on one hand?

# ANSWERS QUIZ 19

1. Short
2. on a map.
3. An adult
4. Snowman.
5. A lighthouse
6. I never said it was raining.
7. Rainbow
8. A telephone
9. A unicorn
10. Normal, you have two hands

# QUIZ 20

1. What is frequently answered even though it has never asked a question?
2. You can give it to someone you love. It is very delicate and can easily be broken. It is, however, sweet and pure and given whole.
3. How many birthdays does the average kid have?
4. It has wings, arrows, diapers and is covered in red.
5. While on my way to St. Ives, I saw a man with his wife. They had seven children and each one had a cat. Each cat had a kitten and each kitten was in a sack. How many people were going to St. Ives?
6. An engineer, an NFL quarterback, and a motorcycle rider enter construction site wearing helmets. Who among the 3 wore the biggest one?
7. What will you find at the end of a rainbow?
8. How can you a ball come back to you after throwing as hard as you can even if there isn't a wall or a floor to bounce it from?
9. If it took four men 24 hours to build a wall, how long would it take two men to build the same wall?
10. What always runs and murmurs silent noises. Owns a bed, but doesn't fall into slumber, has a mouth, but cannot eat?

# ANSWERS QUIZ 20

1.  A doorbell
2.  The heart
3.  One.
4.  A cupid covered with kisses
5.  Just me. I was the only one going to St. Ives
6.  The one with the biggest head, of course!
7.  The end of the rainbow.
8.  Throw it up as high as you can.
9.  No one can build the same wall, because the wall is already built.
10. River

# QUIZ 21

1. There are two birds in front of two other birds. There are two birds behind two other birds. There are two birds beside two other birds. How many birds are there?
2. Zombies, Mummies, Vampires and witches all have one thing in common. What is it?
3. Hi, I'm Rodney and I live on a farm. With me on the farm are 4 other dogs Brownie, Spottie, Whitey, and Blackie. Who is the fifth dog on the farm?
4. Someone dropped an egg on a floor. It didn't break after falling for 2 feet, why?
5. 5 apples were in a basket, how will you divide the five apples for five children so that every child will have an apple while there is an apple that remains in the basket?
6. What has four legs and a back but no body?
7. It can point the way without a hand, always leads the direction. Used in the seas and sand, but always above water, not on land. What is it?
8. I am there when there is light, but I disappear when the shine is on me. What am I?
9. Before going to sleep on your bed, what is the last thing you take off?
10. You don't put me on, but wear me every day, I am changing my color if you leave me out too long. What am I?

# ANSWERS QUIZ 21

1. 4, their position in a square form
2. The letter 'I'
3. Me, Rodney.
4. She drops it higher than two feet, so after it reached the 2nd feet, the egg did not hit the floor yet.
5. 4 children have 1 apple each while the fifth child can have the basket with the remaining apple inside of it.
6. Chair
7. Compass
8. Shadow
9. Your feet. You take them off the floor.
10. Skin

# QUIZ 22

1. I'm the beginning of eternity and at the end of time and space. I am the beginning of every end, and I am the end of every place. What am I?
2. If you do not want bad luck in your life, then you need to avoid this as much as you can, especially at night. It is a very dark creature that is said to bring bad luck to people. What is it?
3. What is even more dangerous than being with a fool?
4. Before Mt. Everest was discovered, what was the tallest mountain in the world? Mt. Everest
5. It is very heavy, almost 5000lbs. It is gray and has the longest nose ever and flies on a broom. What is it?
6. I am an odd number, if you will be taking away a single letter, and I turn into even. What am I?
7. Which candle burns longer? A blue candle or a white candle?
8. What 4-letter hour of the day is spelled the same forwards and backwards?
9. If you purchase a rooster to lay eggs for you and you want to have two eggs daily for breakfast. How many eggs will you have with you after 13 days?
10. Almost everyone loves me. Some love me, but cannot have me since they get allergies from my fur. Those that do not have allergies have me in their houses because I am very friendly. I love sitting by the window at home so that I can watch who comes in and who leaves. When I am excited, I like wagging a certain part of my body. What am I?

# ANSWERS QUIZ 22

1. The letter E
2. A black cat
3. Fooling with a bee
4. Mt. Everest
5. An elephant that is riding on a witch's broomstick
6. Seven
7. Nothing, candle burns shorter, not longer.
8. Noon
9. No eggs, a rooster doesn't lay eggs.
10. A dog

# QUIZ 23

1. Imagine you were at a very strange house. Then suddenly, you hear a very weird sound. You cannot see anything, but I can see you since am floating above you. What am I?

2. It is circular and the bigger it is, the better the girls love it. It can be silver or gold but is always very shiny. Boys give them to their girls as a sign of commitment. To do so, the boy goes down on one knee and slides it on a girl's finger.

3. There were two fathers and two sons who ate eggs for breakfast. They had a meal of three eggs only, but every person received an egg, how was that possible?

4. How can a book with the title that's read as "how to jog" have nothing to do with running?

5. People went to a party and they want to enjoy by the bar. While partying, one of them asked the bartender for 1/2 of beer to drink. While the second one asked for 1/4 pint of beer. Then third person asks for 1/8 of beer and so it goes. Solve how much pints of beer will the bartender needs to give the orders.

6. What vehicle has 4 or more wheels and flies?

7. Kevin flew to Australia at the fantastic speed of a thousand miles per hour. He picked up his friend and flew back, the extra weight caused the plane to only fly 500 miles per hour. What is Kevin's average speed?

8. What do you call a man that lives in disguise, keeps a lot of secrets, and tells nothing but lies? Will you call him a liar? No, because it's his job. He has no choice if he wants to protect the ones he loves. What would you call him?

9. If there are 6 oranges and you take away 4, how many do you have?

10. Which of the football team's players wears the largest helmet?

# ANSWERS QUIZ 23

1.  A ghost
2.  An engagement or a wedding ring
3.  One of the fathers can be considered as a grandfather, then his son, which is also a father, then his own son. There are three of them, the grandfather, the father, and the son.
4.  It's part of an encyclopedia series where the book contains topics starting with the letters HOW up to JOG.
5.  1
6.  A garbage truck.
7.  Kevin flew at 666.67 miles per hour over his entire trip.
8.  He is a spy
9.  Four, because you took four oranges
10. The player with the largest head

# QUIZ 24

1. They are small, brown, blind, very creepy, and only come out at night. They like dark places. What are they?
2. Are you good in math? If so, what is the ratio of a Jack O'lantern's circumference to its diameter?
3. What is it that has a bottom at the top of them?
4. What has leaves, but no branches and a spine, but no bones?
5. How can you tell that a man claiming to have found a coin that was dated 150 B.C. on its face is lying?
6. Penny painted every wall of the cabin. Each wall needed one can of paint. If the cabin had four walls, how many cans of paint did she need? 8, inside and outside.
7. What do dogs have that no other animal has?
8. Why couldn't Goldilocks sleep?
9. What is happening every second, minute, month, and century, but not in every hour, week, year, or decade?
10. A 747 is flying from California to Chicago and crashes on the border of Utah and Colorado. Where will they bury the survivors?

# ANSWERS QUIZ 24

1. Bats
2. It is a pumpkin pie!
3. Your legs
4. A Book
5. B.C. means Before Christ and prior to the birth of Christ, dates weren't conceptualized and used yet. That's why it's impossible for an old coin to be dated 150 B.C. on its face.
6. 8, inside and outside.
7. Puppies.
8. Because of night-bears.
9. Letter N
10. No one died

# QUIZ 25

1. Do they have a 4th of July in Great Britain?
2. There were five soccer teams that were competing and they have to face each other only once. The teams had 2 points each for a win and after the tournament, here is the point table: Manchester UTD was 6, Barcelona was 5, Bayern was 4, Milan was 2, and Real Madrid was unknown. How many points did Real Madrid end up with?
3. How much dirt is there in a hole that is one-foot-deep, one-foot-long and one-foot-wide?
4. Suzy has eight pairs of black gloves and eight pairs of brown gloves in her drawer. In total darkness, how many must she take from that drawer in order to be sure of getting a pair that match?
5. If you don't know me, I am something. If you do, I am considered as nothing and useless. What am I?
6. What is often returned, but never borrowed?
7. What verb or action word reads exactly the same regardless if it's read upright or upside down?
8. What is long, pink and wet and is rude to pull out in front of people?
9. I can cry even if I don't have eyes. I can fly even if I don't have wings. What am I?
10. It always fly, but goes nowhere. What is it?

# ANSWERS QUIZ 25

1. All countries have 4th of July
2. There is a total of ten matches. Tw points were distributed to the winning. Therefore 10 x 2 = 20 points is the sum of all the teams' points. $6 + 5 + 4 + 2 + ? = 20, ? = 3$
3. None, or it wouldn't be a whole
4. Nine.
5. Riddle
6. Thanks
7. SWIMS
8. Tongue
9. A cloud.
10. Flag

# QUIZ 26

1. What's the favorite mode of transportation of rabbits?
2. I am very soft and cuddly, though I look like am grizzly sometimes. Sometimes, I am very big while other times I am just a tiny thing you can hold in your hands. Whatever the size you chose me, I am always stuffed and ready to cuddle you. What am I?
3. The more you take, the more you leave behind. What am I?
4. What falls when thrown up but rises when thrown down?
5. You are participating in a race. If you take the second leading person's place, what position do you finish?
6. Everybody has this and can't lose this. What is it?
7. How much time did a robber get for stealing a calendar?
8. I am a number with three digits. Compared to the ones digit, the digit on the tens is 5 times more while on the hundreds digit, it is 8 less than my tens digit. Guess what number am I.
9. What can be measured but not seen?
10. What increases but never decreases?

# ANSWERS QUIZ 26

1. The hare-plane.
2. A teddy bear
3. Footsteps
4. Ball
5. If you take the second runner's place, you arrive second.
6. A shadow.
7. 12 months (there are 12 months in a calendar).
8. 194
9. Time
10. Your age

# QUIZ 27

1. Just before you go to sleep every night, you tell me what to do. Every morning before you wake, I do what I am told, yet I can never escape your scold. What am I?
2. I can move quickly, but I have no legs. My skin will shed, but I stay the same. I can sound like bacon frying and I am hatched from an egg. What am I?
3. There is a man who lives on the top floor of a 24-floor apartment building. Every day he rides the elevator down to the first floor and then he walks to work. When he comes home, he rides the elevator halfway up and uses the stairs to get to the top floor. He does this every day unless there is someone in the elevator with him. Why?
4. If there are two twins, three triplets, and four quintuplets, how many people are there?
5. What was the favorite thing for ghosts to do on Saturday night?
6. I am a source of happiness for many, but I am also a source of sorrow for many. I grow very fast, way fast that most people do not realize when I do. But, I die very slow. Depending on some people and situations, I can be a great pain or great joy.
7. It is a popular place, but no one ever wants to be there. Woe unto you if you are stuck there. It is full of many scary ghosts. Where is this place?
8. I always stay in the corner as I travel around the world. What am I?
9. Where do mummies and zombies go when they are very exhausted from working?
10. I'm the start of awesome. You can find me at the end of a comma. I'm also in the middle of a stomach. What am I?

# ANSWERS QUIZ 27

1.  An alarm clock
2.  A snake
3.  The man was too short to reach the button for the top floor. If someone was with him, then he would ask them to push it. His only other choice was to press the highest button he could reach and use the stairs to get to the top floor.
4.  Two twins are already 2 people, same as the rest. Therefore $2 + 3 + 4 = 9$.
5.  They loved to Boogie
6.  A relationship
7.  The haunted house
8.  Stamp
9.  They always take a coffin break
10. Letter A

# QUIZ 28

1. Imagine that you are in a ferry boat located in the middle of the Caspian Sea. Suddenly, your boat becomes surrounded by two whales and a shark. They're circling your boat and are about to eat you alive! What are you going to do to stop this? Answer: You should stop imagining!
2. Which weighs more – a pound of rocks or a pound of cotton balls? They are of the same weight, they weigh a pound.
3. What has two heads, four eyes, six legs, and a tail?
4. You can neither see nor touch me. You cannot even feel me, but I can cook a meal for you. What am I?
5. Why would witches buy magazines?
6. There was a contest in a beach resort to guess the number of beach balls inside the net bag. Pearl guessed 20, Alex guessed 21, James guessed 22, Dick guessed 17 and Adam guessed 16. There was only one that was correct, the others were off by: 4, 3, 1, and 2. How many beach balls were there?
7. What object allows you to literally see through walls?
8. You are hearing a conversation between three people. Even though you're close enough to hear everything they're saying, you can only hear two voices. What must the other person be doing?
9. When did New Year's Day and Christmas day fall on the same year?
10. The more of these you take, the more you leave behind. What are they? Footsteps

# ANSWERS QUIZ 28

1. You should stop imagining.
2. They are of the same weight, they weigh a pound.
3. Cowboy riding his horse
4. A microwave particle.
5. So that they can read all the horoscopes
6. 20
7. A window
8. He is listening.
9. Every year!
10. Footsteps

# QUIZ 29

1. How do you know if a cat burglar has broken into your house?
2. What is put on a table, cut, but never eaten?
3. I am alive even without air to breathe, I am cold as ice. I am never thirsty, but I will forever be drinking. What am I?
4. What can travel the whole way around the world while staying in the very same corner?
5. I never ask questions but am always answered. What am I?
6. He is very old, has a long white beard, and gives out the best presents. But, on Halloween day we all forget him. Who is he?
7. What has a body made of glass and a neck but no head?
8. What word In the English language is always spelled wrong?
9. You can catch it, but not throw it? What is it?
10. How can you make your car not a car?

# ANSWERS QUIZ 29

1. Your cat is missing
2. Deck
3. Fish
4. A postage stamp
5. Doorbell
6. Santa Claus
7. A bottle.
8. Wrong
9. Cold
10. Turn it (take a turn) into a parking lot.

# QUIZ 30

1. What is the symbol in mathematics that you can put between 5 and 9 to have a number that is greater than 5, but smaller than 9?
2. What has a neck and no head, two arms but no hands?
3. Most animals and creatures grow up, but which creatures grow down?
4. A man is sitting in his cabin. Hours after he gets out of his cabin and was already in a whole new place. How is this possible?
5. Why do birds fly south for the winter?
6. What can you make that you can't see?
7. What should you do when you see a little green man?
8. You have 20 apples in a basket, 20 children come to ask for one each, and you will want to give all the apples to each of them, but still keep one inside the basket? How will you do it?
9. John was ordered to paint the numbers one through one hundred on one hundred apartments. How many times is he going to paint 8?
10. What always goes to bed with his shoes on?

# ANSWERS QUIZ 30

1. A decimal point. 5.9
2. Shirt
3. Geese (Down feathers)
4. He is a pilot and airplanes have cabins
5. It's too far to walk.
6. Noise
7. Cross the road
8. Give 19 apples to 19 children out of 20 of them and give the basket to the last child with the apple in it.
9. 20 times, count all the 8 at the ends, from 8 until 98.
10. Horse

# QUIZ 31

1. Even if it rains harder, it doesn't become any wetter than when it rained lighter. What is it?
2. How would you divide 55 such that one number is equivalent to 1.5 times of the other? What are those numbers?
3. What starts with the letter "t", is filled with "t" and ends in "t"?
4. How do you pay dog catchers?
5. What is above the queen?
6. What can point in every direction but cannot reach any destination by itself?
7. When is it OK to go on red and stop at green?
8. What grows only upwards and can never come down?
9. People buy me and still disturb me for more than 1 hours 30 minutes- What am I?
10. A red house is constructed using red bricks. A sky blue house was built using blue bricks. A yellow house is built out of yellow bricks. How is a greenhouse built?

# ANSWERS QUIZ 31

1. Water.
2. 22 and 33.
3. Teapot.
4. By the "pound".
5. Her crown
6. The compass
7. When you're eating a watermelon
8. Height
9. Football
10. It's made with glass.

# QUIZ 32

1. You will find a hundred of this in the graveyard. But, in this you will not find any dead bodies. You will, however, find all the information about all the dead bodies in each burial place.
2. How can you place a pencil on the floor of a room so that no one can jump over it?
3. A Dracula will draw and bank this item. What is it?
4. What has two hands but is unable to clap?
5. Often talked of but never seen. Always coming but never here. It sounds like an idea, but it is just a dream. Still approaching and coming near. You close your eyes, hoping to see me soon. But when you wake up, you realize I'm as far out of your reach as the moon
6. In the ground it's nothing, but give it time and it'll be something. What is it?
7. Ghosts have a favorite spot on the road that they always want to travel at. Which is it?
8. The day before two days after the day before tomorrow is Saturday. What day is it today?
9. How do you spell Candy in just two letters?
10. What is the thing which, once poured out, cannot be gathered again?

# ANSWERS QUIZ 32

1. A tombstone
2. You can put it next to the wall.
3. Blood
4. A clock
5. The future
6. Seed
7. The dead-end
8. Friday
9. C and Y c (and) y
10. Rain

# QUIZ 33

1. What number do you get when you multiply all of the numbers on a telephone's number pad?
2. Why did the vampire enroll in the art school?
3. What can you find on a fish, in music, or under your bathroom sink?
4. Who is the fastest human being who ever lived?
5. What did the ghost order as desert when he went to the restaurant?
6. What type of Jack has a head but no body?
7. This can make ten octopuses laugh. What is it? Ten tickles. (Sounds like "tentacles.")
8. A night watchman, while on patrol at night, dreams that the king will die in a plane crash due to the love he has for the king he quickly tells him in the morning, but the king tells him to not worry. He flies away and when he returns from the trip, he fires the night watchman. Why does the king fire the night watchman?
9. Sometimes I tend to shine, at times I am dull, I can be big, and I can be small. I can be pointy as well as curved. But don't ask me any questions because I am not smart enough to answer you even if I am sharp. So, what am I?
10. I am a human being I walk with 4 legs, what am I?

# ANSWERS QUIZ 33

1. You get 0, because there is 0 on the telephone and if you multiply any number with 0, you get 0.
2. He wanted to be taught how to draw blood
3. Scales
4. Adam. It's because he was first person ever of the human race.
5. An ice scream
6. A jack-o-lantern.
7. Ten Tickles (sounds like "tentacles")
8. Because he knew that the watchman was sleeping during his duty, that's why he had dreams.
9. A knife.
10. A baby

# QUIZ 34

1. What happens once in soccer, twice in football, but never once in baseball?
2. I am found in the quietest, yet very creepy place. For people to come in, they have to die first. What am I?
3. I don't have it when I share it and when I don't share it, I keep it. What's that?
4. Jasper went on a hike in the forest. He took something and left something. He did not leave anything behind, though, and did not have anything more with him when he left. What happened? He took photographs and left footprints.
5. Mat's mom had a lot of children. She had twelve in total. Their names are January, February, March, April, May, June, July, August, September, and November. What was the last child's name?
6. It takes four people four hours to repair four bicycles. So, how many bicycles can eight people repair in about eight hours?
7. I may be cracked, sometimes chapped and even pale. However, there is one thing that is always constant; am always very soft, full and sometimes red. I am always shared between special people. Sometimes, with strangers but that is not always a good idea.
8. There are two ropes that one happens to be 2 yards shorter, but is three times longer than the first rope. How long is it?
9. What occurs four times in every week, twice in every month, only once in a year but never in a day?
10. It comes in Orange, it is very hollow and very smart. What is it?

# ANSWERS QUIZ 34

1. The letter "O"
2. A cemetery
3. A secret.
4. He took photographs and left footprints.
5. The last child was named Mat
6. 16 bicycles.
7. Lips
8. If the length of the rope plus two yards = three times the length of the rope, then the rope is one-yard long
9. Letter E
10. A bright Jack O'lantern

# QUIZ 35

1. You're asleep in bed when you hear your neighbor pounding on the front door, asking for some jam, which is in a jar, inside a box, inside the refrigerator. What do you open first? Your eyes

2. What are you certain to find inside your pocket when you reach into it?

3. It is a very common little bug. However, even though it is so small, most people fear it so much. There is a name for this fear. It is called arachnophobia. Who is this little guy?

4. They are very colorful flowers and have a beautiful fragrance. They also have little ones. What type are they?

5. What goes through a door but never goes in. And never comes out?

6. I always grow. I need air even if I don't have lungs and water kills me, what am I?

7. What is the three-digit number, including its decimal point, will give you the same exact answer either you subtract or divide it by five?

8. Why did the student eat his homework?

9. I will make mountains crumble and temples fall. I've been here since the beginning, and I'll be here long after the end. No one can escape me, and some will say they don't have enough of me. What am I?

10. They lived in the northern and southern areas. Those were the good ones. The bad ones, who were not liked by anyone, came from the eastern and the western areas. They all flew in broomsticks. Who are they?

# ANSWERS QUIZ 35

1. Your eyes
2. Hand
3. A spider
4. Orchids
5. Keyhole
6. Fire
7. 6.25
8. Because the teacher told him, it was a piece of cake.
9. Time
10. Witches

# QUIZ 36

1. I can make you cry; make the dead live and form you smile, I can relive the past and reverse time. I form in a single second, but I last a life time. What am I?
2. What is pronounced as one letter, written with three, and is the same forwards and backwards? Eye
3. What number comes next in the sequence? 1, 6, 13, 22, 33, ?
4. Where do ghosts, mummies and zombies love to go swimming?
5. I am either something's mother or a father, but haven't given a birth. I am not always still, but I never wander. What am I?
6. We are flowers, but not ordinary flowers. We can French kiss and even smooch. What kind of flowers are we?
7. What seven-letter word becomes eight when you remove 2 letters from it?
8. I have 5 letters, when you remove my first letter, it's considered as a taboo, if you take away my first and last letters, it can become a genre of music. What am I?
9. There are two airplanes in the sky. One plane is from New York to London with the speed of 600 Mph. While the other plane comes from London to New York with a speed of 500 Mph. If both of the plane meet, which will be closer to London?
10. What is between heaven and earth?

# ANSWERS QUIZ 36

1. Memory
2. Eye
3. 46. Add 2 and the difference between the previous numbers to the last number.
4. The Dead Sea
5. Tree
6. Tulip flowers
7. The living room.
8. Grape
9. They will be the same distance away when they meet.
10. And

# QUIZ 37

1. I can save a memory forever, but fire can end my life. I've been around for a while, but I probably won't go out of style. What am I?
2. What made the game warden arrest the ghost?
3. What instrument did the skeleton play?
4. What has thirteen hearts, but no body or soul?
5. How do you tell which witch is the witch?
6. Summer is here, so I'm wearing green. When fall comes, I change into yellow. When winter comes, I'll get rid of my covers. What am I?
7. I am a body; I have a head, arms and head. However, I always look naked. Guess who I am.
8. I am a figure of speech, but I don't say the truth- What am I?
9. She is very beautiful and very famous. She is very flexible and can be anything you want her to be. People of different tastes will go after her because she can be different and fit for everyone's taste. She knows people have different tastes, so she comes with different colors and different sizes. Sometimes, she has long hair while other times she has short hair. Sometimes she is a blonde while other times she is a brunette. She can rock straight or curly hair and comfortably fit in your hands. Who is she?
10. A man got a $15 haircut. Using a $20 bill, he paid the barber but the barber had no change. The barber went to the flower shop and converted the $20 bill for a $10-dollar bill and two $5 bills. He gave $5 to the man for his change. The lady confronted the barber later, and told him that the $20 bill he gave her was falsified. The barber agreed, and gives another $20 bill to the lady. He tries to figure out how much money he'd lost later that day. How much did he lose?

# ANSWERS QUIZ 37

1. A picture
2. His haunting license had long expired
3. Trombone
4. Playing cards
5. You can never tell the difference because they are twin witches
6. A tree (with leaves)
7. A Skeleton
8. Irony
9. Barbie doll
10. He lost 5$ and gave a free haircut, since the lady gave him $20, but got 20$ back and the man who earned the haircut gave the barber no money, but earned $5.

# QUIZ 38

1. What flies forever, Rests never?
2. What has only one eye but still can't see?
3. What has a head, but can't think and has no limbs but can drive?
4. What happens when you cross a teacher and a Dracula?
5. Which is heavier, a ton of steel or 2 tons of feathers?
6. I am a flying creature and very colorful, but no, I am not a rainbow. I am a very social creature and I know I am very beautiful, but I am not a human being. Who am I?
7. Throw a ball 10 meters away from you, how can you have it back without hitting anything?
8. Black cats are said to be bad luck. But, when is the one time you are guaranteed of bad luck when you cross the black cat?
9. Abigail took an exam that had twenty questions. The total grade was calculated by giving ten points for every correct answer and deducting five points for each wrong answer. Abigail answered all twenty questions and earned a remark of 125. Solve how many wrong answers she had.
10. One day, Alice asks John: "If I gave you two soccer balls, and then two other soccer balls, how many soccer balls would you have?" John replies: I would have 5. Alice says: "No, John. If I have two soccer balls, and then you give me two more soccer balls, how many would I have?". To which John replies: "4.". "That's right. Now, if I gave you 2 soccer balls, and then other 2 soccer balls, how many would you have?". John replies: "5.". It seems that John is wrong, but actually, he isn't. Why can we say that?

# ANSWERS QUIZ 38

1. Wind
2. A needle
3. Hammer
4. You get blood tests
5. The feathers. It's because it's 2 tons compared to only 1 ton of steel.
6. Butterfly
7. Throw it upwards.
8. When you are a mouse
9. If Abigail got perfect score, she would have earned 200. Since she only scored 125, there is the missing 75 points. Each incorrect answer means losing a total of 15 points (10 for not having the correct answer and 5 for answering incorrectly) 75 divided by 15 is 5.
10. He already has one.

# QUIZ 39

1. What is flat, usually square, and made from trees but isn't wood?
2. Nightly they come without being fetched, what are they?
3. Most girls cannot go out without it. It makes them feel more beautiful. It is something that you apply on your body, lips and face.
4. Amy's mother had five children. She named the first Tuesday. The second was named Wednesday. The third was named Thursday. The fourth was named Friday. What was the name of the fifth child? Answer: Amy!
5. A man shaves several times a day, yet he still has a beard. How is this possible?
6. During the day of his execution, a power outage occurs, and the prisoner in question is led to a room where he will live his last moments. He's been given the opportunity to choose the method of execution. He is shown an electric chair and a crocodile. Which method does the man have to choose to survive?
7. What building holds the most stories?
8. I help old people, I have a name of a bird, and I feed cargos on ships. I am not alive. What am I?
9. I am a very stubborn creature who loves jumping from one tree to another. I have a long tail that I love to swing back and forth with whenever I am thinking of something serious. My favorite meals are fruits, nuts and some certain types of seeds. I have some features of a human being, but I am not one. What am I?
10. What word has only one letter, which begins and ends with the letter E?

# ANSWERS QUIZ 39

1. Paper
2. Stars
3. Make-up
4. Amy.
5. He is a barber
6. Electric chair, since there is no electricity, he won't be executed.
7. A library
8. Crane
9. A monkey
10. Envelope, it starts and ends with "E" and contains just one letter inside.

# QUIZ 40

1. What is never eaten before lunch?
2. What kind of frog can jump higher than a building?
3. What gets bigger the more you take away from it?
4. They live in houses as pets. It is said that they have more lives than any other creature. They are fluffy and sometimes want to be cuddled, while other times they just want to be left alone. They can be super active or super lazy. What are they?
5. I have three letters in my name. I am green and a seed. Remove two letters and I still sound the same. What am I?
6. Mr. Jones has 2 children; if the older child is a boy what is the probability that the younger child is a boy?
7. I am a body part. In fact, I am two. I share the same name as a type of length, and I fit inside shoes. What am I?
8. It sleeps during the day but dances in the night with a bright light. It comes out at night to party and provide light to its guests at the party. What is it?
9. What needs to be taken from you before you have it?
10. I know everything you know, but I am the same size as your hand. What am I?

# ANSWERS QUIZ 40

1. Dinner
2. Any frog because buildings can't jump
3. Hole
4. A cat
5. Pea
6. 50%
7. Feet
8. A candle
9. Picture
10. I am your brain